What Matters

What Matters

*spiritual nourishment
for head and heart*

Frederick Franck

with illustrations by the author

Walking Together, Finding the Way
SKYLIGHT PATHS Publishing
Woodstock, Vermont

What Matters: Spiritual Nourishment for Head and Heart

2004 First SkyLight Paths Printing
Text and art © 1993 by Frederick Franck

Library of Congress Cataloging-in-Publication Data
Franck, Frederick, 1909–
What matters: spiritual nourishment for head and heart / by Frederick Franck
p.   cm.
Originally published: A Little Compendium on that Which Matters. New York:
St. Martin's, 1993.
ISBN 1-59473-013-X (hardcover)
1. Spiritual life. I. Title.
BL624 .F725 2004
204'.32—dc22

                                                                    2003022667

SkyLight Paths Publishing is creating a place where people of different spiritual traditions come together for challenge and inspiration, a place where we can help each other
understand the mystery that lies at the heart of our existence.

SkyLight Paths sees both believers and seekers as a community that increasingly transcends traditional boundaries of religion and denomination—people wanting to learn
from each other, *walking together, finding the way.*

Manufactured in Canada

SkyLight Paths, "Walking Together, Finding the Way" and colophon are trademarks of
LongHill Partners, Inc., registered in the U.S. Patent and Trademark Office.

Walking Together, Finding the Way
Published by SkyLight Paths Publishing
A Division of LongHill Partners, Inc.
Sunset Farm Offices, Route 4, P.O. Box 237
Woodstock, VT 05091
Tel (802) 457-4000   Fax (802) 457-4004
www.skylightpaths.com

Directions for use:

This little compendium, not to be confused with currently fashionable spiritual divertissements, is the organic extract of long and intense, mostly non-discursive rumination. It is hoped to act as an enzyme activating similar rumination in carefully (self-) selective subjects. Redundancies have not been filtered out of this distillate since they are an integral constituent of the ruminating process; slight cloudiness therefore is normal and harmless.

As this product is free from artificial flavoring and coloring, it may not be readily absorbable by the average conditioned ruminatory system. For most cases the initial optimum dose consists of three or four ruminations at one time, as the active ingredients are released gradually. Once the desired blood level has been established, dosage may be adapted to taste.

Warning:

May cause drowsiness, in which case dosage should be reduced immediately. Side effects are mild: minor headaches and oscillations in blood pressure have been reported. In case of accidental overdose, intake should be discontinued at once and the habitual dose of T.V. administered as a counter irritant.

If on the other hand a ruminatory chain reaction should occur, it should not be interfered with, as toxicity is minimal.

Zuigan used to call out to himself:

"Zuigan, are you there?"

"Yes, Master!"

"Are you awake?"

"Yes, Master!"

"Really awake?"

"Oh, yes!"

"And so you won't let yourself be bamboozled, confused, side-tracked again?"

"No, Master! Never!"

What is all too easily dismissed as "anti-intellectualism" may well be the tendency, in extremis, to reestablish some balance between thinking and feeling, between the activities of the right and left hemispheres (was perhaps the right one formerly known as "the heart"?...) after a few centuries of that heartless cerebrality which culminated in the perfect technological know-how to prepare our demise.

In what follows it is blandly assumed that, however enigmatic, there *is* a Reality/Truth, a Tao, a "really-Real" which transcends the crudely empirical, that there *is* Meaning to our sojourn on earth and that we may even be able to grasp this Meaning or be grasped by it.

Could the Meaning of being born human be, to become Human?

The illusion that discursive thinking may establish contact with transcendent Reality/Truth was an ingredient of Western culture long before Descartes imagined he was, just because he thought. This is not a plea against thinking, but for another kind of thinking, that "non-thinking thinking" which includes human intuition and feeling.

It is a plea for a logic in which the absolutely relative and the absolutely Absolute do not necessarily clash, nor are even separated, in which it is not "either this or that," but perhaps "both this and that" or "neither this nor that" which approaches the really Real.

When logic follows experience, it is likely to be valid. When experience derives from logic, it is bound to be self-deception: delusional, spurious, false.

The criteria of what it means to be fully Human, which Lao Tze, Chuang Tzu, Gautama Buddha and Jesus Christ essentially shared, remained vital as long as the movements rooted in their lives and their words remained vital, namely until the rise of modern Nihilism. The social, economic, political premises of modern Nihilism are based on the outworn mechanical world view of 19th-century science in its anti-human hubris. The Tao of being Human is denied.

In the Mahayana Buddhist tradition the paradigm of the fully Human is *explicitly* stated: the transhistorical Buddha is manifest as "Buddha Nature," the "Original Face," Rinzai's "True Man," as that which lies hidden as the spiritual core in everyone born human, waiting to be realized. In contemporary language one might interpret it as being the "Specifically Human" latent in everyone born human.

The Christian tradition allowed
Jesus—as paradigm of this Specifically
Human, as the Christ—to remain *implicit,*
overgrown with theological and legalistic
foliage. When at times a mystic made "The
Light of the World," the transhistorical, the
Cosmic Christ, too explicit by stressing
the "Sleeping Christ within," he did so at
risk of the pyre. A Mahayana Christianity
in which the emphasis is based on "The
Light that lighteneth every man come into
the world" is overdue indeed.

A consensus between the religious
traditions on the nature of the
Transcendent/Immanent is, of course,
unattainable. Nor is it indispensable.
There is, however, a remarkable conver-
gence in Christianity, Judaism, Buddhism,
Sufism *on the criteria of what deserves to be
called "Human"* and what is less than
human, what is pre-human, in-human,
sub-human, anti-human, even sub-animal.

Where these criteria have remained all too implicit, they must at last be made clearly explicit and shouted from the housetops, as the basis of a vital transcultural, transreligious spirituality, so desperately needed. *The emphatic consensus on what it really means to be Human reopens the perspective, indicates the Way towards a once more liveable world.*

The religious traditions also share the insight that the pre-condition for becoming fully Human, as well as for attaining full awakening to Reality/Truth, is the relativisation, the overcoming of the empirical ego's narcissism, its delusions of supremacy.

The words "spiritual," "spirituality" have been so thoroughly cheapened that a moratorium on their misuse is overdue.

11

D. T. Suzuki wrote that the spiritual life is pain raised above the level of mere sensation. *Spirituality, born from life-pain, is that specifically human impulse from delusion to the really-Real within and outside of ourselves,* which characterizes the maturation of the human inner process: the thrust towards, and the commitment to, the Real.

Authentic spirituality is intimately related to firsthand, direct experiencing. It may mature through various disciplines, as for instance structured meditation and verbalized prayer. To live in radical openness to pure experiencing in kitchen, bedroom, subway, newspaper, that is: to everyday life, inside as well as around oneself may, however, be the equivalent of both formal meditation and verbal prayer. It is the finding of one's path without being "bamboozled, confused, sidetracked," at every step.

Anything labeled "spirituality" that is not experiential, intimately related to direct experiencing, is therefore highly suspect of being pseudo-spirituality, self-indulgence, yet another parlor game.

Some symptoms by which pseudo-spirituality may be recognized are: sentimentality, premature group formation, proselytizing, fanaticism, holier-than-thou delusions, superstitions, spiritual tourism. Above all: unconcern, detachment from all the avoidable suffering, injustice, violence constantly being inflicted on the great majority of our fellow humans.

Pseudo-spirituality is not only offered for sale, it is marketed wholesale, retail and successfully franchised. It can be ordered from dozens of mail order catalogs, or consumed on location, *à la carte.* I copy the following from the one I received today:

"... X's hilarious style could irreparably alter you. He'll gently escort you on a celestial journey, retracing the billions of years of cosmic evolution ... into life and consciousness.... Master Y will transform your relationships into reflections of holiness and joy.... You'll leave here with mind full of new ideas, body full of wonderful food spiced ... with lots of laughter and fun relaxation...."

To objectify spirituality, to make it the object of "study" is almost equally absurd: it is the very wellspring of all valid art, culture, science and of all humanly valid political and economic structures.

Spirituality then originates and matures in the individual person, but not remaining limited to that person, it has inevitable social, interpersonal effects, even if only restricted to one's immediate surroundings. In essence: awakening from the empirical ego's narcissistic delusions, above all liberation from the illusion of Otherness, insight into the hallucinatory nature of the little "Me!," of Us versus Them.

The Word, Logos, Tao, is not an ingredient of Being. It is That of which beings, things, events are the manifestations, of which all are in-carnations during their existence-time.

Carl Jung says that a person who fails to attain a religious attitude toward existence itself remains infantile, hence pathological.

The religious attitude to existence is rooted in wonder at the mystery of sheer Being, at being here at all, the axiomatic certainty that there is a Meaning in our being here, hence in total openness to It.

Both the institutional religions which in their infantile egocentricity turn their insights into the Mystery they proclaim upside down, this and the psychopathology of our pitiless, arrogant secularized society, are incompatible with religious attitude to existence.

What for the "Realpolitiker," the Naive Realist, is "real," is sheer illusion. It denies the crucially important: the reality of every human life as an inner process between birth and death. It is their rash little dance on the thin ice that covers the precipice of Nothingness.

The delusion that we live forever, the disregard of our certain death, poisons all planning; all targets are perpetually missed, resulting in uninterrupted chains of catastrophe.

"People make faces as if they were going to live forever" says an ancient Japanese senryu.

The man-eating myth misnomered "History" is the eternal replay of the six o'clock news, made up of mayhem, bloodletting, disaster, half-truths, inanity and nonsense about the powerful, the celebrities; all products of that Naive Realism for which the Dow replaces the Tao.

That our lethal problems of war, hunger and violence are of a political, economic, technological nature and hence can be solved by political, economic, technological sleight of hand, is the dominant superstition of the Naive Realist. They are however problems of Reality/Truth, hence cannot be solved without an insight into this Reality/Truth in relation to human destiny. They require the religious attitude to existence/ non-existence.

In our time the survival of the religious institutions and their traditional structures is of minor importance compared with the survival of a religious orientation to life-as-such. Without it, life-as-such is in mortal jeopardy.

Poverty may be quite compatible with a religious attitude to existence; destitution, hunger, utter humiliation, negate it. Avoidable suffering is one of the great crimes perpetrated on the majority of the human race, and the frightful karma that weighs on our and future generations.

That we are not the masters but the vulnerable products of this earth is the elementary insight. Without it all contemporary forms of "spirituality" show their irrelevancy and mendacity.

This insight into the real place of ourselves, and our planet, in the fabric of the cosmic Whole is integral to any contemporary religious orientation to existence. The anthropocentric (read: ego-centric) worldview has become as untenably anti-scientific as it is anti-religious. It distorts all perceptions of our reality-situation and voids all our scenarios for adequate action, justifies coercion as permissible.

Hwa Yen (Chinese), Kegon (Japanese), Avatamsaka (Sanskrit), probably the highest expression of Buddhist thought/intuition formulated—as early as the 7th century—the infinite continuum of mutually inter-dependent phenomena in the universe, even their mutual interpenetration. Each one of the phenomena—or beings—in this continuum is at once free to be totally itself, yet totally interwoven with all others.

Alfred North Whitehead, although un-familiar with Hwa Yen, posited the "mutual immanence" of all phenomena.

Hwa Yen's "One in One, One in All, All in One, All in All" foreshadows not only our belated ecological awareness, but also that global, macro-ecological and macro-ecumenical "spirituality" without which a viable world order is sheer eyewash. Its view of Totality embodies the very essence of the religious attitude to all Being/Non-Being.

The Oneness of the Many, the Manyness of the One, the total interdependence of all that lives on earth, far from being an eschatological pipe dream, is the fundamental *fact* we disregard at the price of inevitable extinction. It is hard to visualize an authentic contemporary "spirituality"—as relationship to the Real—without this insight into a "sacred" ecology. The responsibilities that follow from this "sacred" ecology are incompatible with "The Economy" venerated as sacrosanct.

Werner Heisenberg at the end of his life said: "Science is no longer so important, man is important." If the religious institutions were to adopt a parallel attitude, they would at once recoup their relevancy.

To whomsoever the Human is important, the Earth is of prime importance and hence the organic unity of what is as infinitely diversified as it is interdependent. It is the radical corollary to Albert Schweitzer's principle of "Reverence for Life."

"All men are one man, one man is all men," says a Sutra. Indeed, the plural of man does not exist. This however, does not make us into "equals." It makes us aware of being absolutely equivalent, however unequal....

The collision of the empirical ego in its delusions with the unyielding wall of the Real is the inescapable moment of Truth in every human life. It leaves us with two options: either to awaken to the Reality of the human condition, and proceed towards ultimate integration, or to flounder towards terminal disintegration. When all devices have failed, all escape hatches are closed, the moment of metanoia is at hand.

Ego ("I am, you aren't, they aren't"), the con-committant of *avidya,* primordial ignorance, in Buddhism (and of *the Fall* in Judeo-Christianity), is by nature ruthless, violent. The collective or in-group ego is— as intrinsically—mass-murderous.

Unless the liberation from the delusions and follies of the empirical ego coincides with the liberation from the collective hallucinations of the group-ego of nation, gender, church, race, tribe, we remain caught in ever more evil compulsions, all of them equally anti-human.

"All that burns in hell is ego," says Tauler. One might add: all that proves incombustible in hell is Christ/Nature, Buddha/Nature—for hell is of the making of ego.

Where all intuitions of value, of a Cosmic Order, of transcendent Meaning are dismissed as fancies, we flounder into the folly and vileness of an unrelieved nightmare.

Glib talk about the necessity of "killing the ego" is to be distrusted. The development of ego is an indispensable phase of the human voyage. To "kill it" before it has matured, is as questionable an operation as any other abortion.

It may not be a matter of "killing the ego" at all, but of attaining an existential, a total insight into its merciless, unbounded narcissism. Where ego boasts or imagines to have "killed," "overcome" ego, the very depth of delusion has been reached.

The Christ event does not point at the improvement, the ennoblement of ego, but at its crucifixion. Metanoia is not the utter refinement, and hence the safe-guarding of ego, but insight into its illusoriness and the total turnabout away from it: the rediscovery of the "Original Face," the True Self. The perfected ego is one of the most evil idols ever created.

The True Self is the Specifically Human we have genetically in common and is no one's private domain.

Jesus as crutch for the ego is that mortally dangerous fundamentalist totem with two heads, one human, one divine, of which the history is extremely bloody, neither human nor divine.

Ego looks, looks out for itself, but is blind as a bat. When I SEE I am all eye; ego is momentarily forgotten, I am nothing but a focus of awareness. "The Meaning of Life is to SEE," said Hui Neng, and another master: "I am not worried about what you *do,* how you conduct your life, for I approve of how you *see.*"

To glimpse things and beings as they are in themselves, as if from their center, is to see oneself as one is in one's own center.

Redemption is the liberation from the obsessions of the isolated "Me" encapsulated in its bag of skin, locus of our almost unconquerable hallucinations. The Christ, the Buddha overcame it, lived and died as if to prove that it is, after all, possible.

Hence they are the Lodestars by which we can set our life-course to the fulfillment of the Human Way, of the inner human process. They are the Beacons by which we can estimate, be aware of, the distance that still separates us from it.

One might call "Grace" that ever present, be it latent, potential of insight into the "Unborn," the "True Self," St. John's "Light that lighteneth every man," Rinzai's "True Man in this mass of red flesh": into the Tao of being Human.

Just as ego cannot overcome ego, karma cannot liberate us from karma. The Buddha, however, reminds us that there is something *Unborn,* un-conditioned in us, without which we would be powerless to liberate ourselves from what is born and conditioned, points at that which is the Specifically Human in us.

However many millions of us are born, each one embodies the Unborn. This is the magna carta of each one's inviolability, each one's full human dignity.

When the encapsulated ego opens itself ever so little, be it to the outside or the inside, compassion, wisdom, agapè, sophia, become visible, hence attainable.

 When the Christ says: "'Follow Me," he says "Follow that Unborn.... It is within you."

 Hui Hai, 9th century, says: "Your treasure house is within you, it contains all you'll ever need..., " and Thomas' Gospel: "The Kingdom is within you *and* around you."

 Karma, the chain of cause and effect, is not linearly linked, neither is it limited to the narrowly personal. The linkage is transpersonal, genetic, as in a limitless net of which all mazes are interconnected in all dimensions of time and space. Product of numberless ancestors: "they" and "we," from moment to moment, live in symbiosis with the untold others.

Going back a mere five hundred years: you and I each have a pedigree including some 100,000 forebears. A thousand years ago, it numbered some hundred million humans! The proud male-transmitted "family name," adorned perhaps 0.01% of our "legitimate" ancestors. Related to every single being that lives on earth, our identity is: to be Human ... no more, no less, and even that only potentially! All self-labeling, ethnic, religious, national is pitifully ludicrous.

I wonder: who will read this Compendium through to the end? Perhaps, out of a feeling of fraternity, you or some other fellow marginal, equally dissatisfied with all acquisitions, material and "spiritual," all pretensions of belonging to some elite or other, and who like myself refuses all self-labeling.

The true status we share is that of being a hollow tube that breathes, eats, excretes automatically, and yet contains that Unborn that has a tiny little voice, sometimes faintly heard, mostly mute. Then it sits in a corner of the tube and weeps.

The derelict asleep on the pavement under a jute sack is disquieting, because he is me, after the always possible catastrophe! We were both lovely babies last week, aggressive teenagers yesterday, the corpses of tomorrow morning....

To be aware of still breathing (until it stops), of the earth (as long as it lasts), of feeling hungry and delighted with a fresh egg, a piece of still warm bread, is to be still part of humanity.

Human community is inconceivable unless founded in the Specifically Human and a value system based on it. The *en masse* progression of humans to Teilhard's point Omega seems a touching optical illusion. Each one has his hands full, a whole life long, to get close to it. Once touched, the hell from where one escaped, is seen for what it is.

The metanoia, the turnabout at the base that reveals the Specifically Human as the True Self, at once makes one belong to that one human community, that Sangha, that "Mystical Body of Christ" that is independent from all Institutions.

One can go on earning a living and yet refuse to identify with the aims, the anti-human delusions of this society, to regress to its by now necrotic, slogans, its "progress." To be aware that to escape it is as illusory in the Himalayas as it is in

Brooklyn, but that there are still options
for more or less right livelihood,
simplification of life aims and even
compassionate action according to one's
capacity, circumstance, temperament....

How?

Each one must find these options for
himself.

What for lack of a better term I call
"The New Order" is the anonymous,
unorganized, organic network of awareness
beyond all ideological labels, born under
the lash of anxiety on the threshold of our
collective suicide. It is a network of loners,
encompassing those who reflect on the
meaning of being Human in our tech-
notronic rat trap, who dare to fathom the
depths of life, of death, in order to attain a
life-praxis, an ethos suitable for this end-
time: a religious orientation to existence.
Without badge, without watchword, they
recognize, hearten one another.

The word "faith" in the Christian context of Western culture has the connotation of a personal relationship with and commitment to God. In this Compendium it is used in the sense of an existential commitment to Reality/Truth and Will to Meaning. Faith, as such, is a constant human constituent. "As a man's faith is, so is he," says the Bhagavad Gita.

"Belief" is one of the expressions of faith. It implies assent to dogmatic propositions on someone else's authority. Beliefs therefore may be a hurdle to direct experience, to intuitive perception of Reality/Truth. Mark Twain's schoolboy who interpreted: "Faith is to believe what you know ain't so" confused faith with belief.

Faith is the Specifically Human constituent and "beliefs" are the forms it assumes at certain stages of spiritual development. Beliefs are time- and culture-bound.

Each one of Jesus' great words:
"I and My Father are One" (not-two...!)
"Who has seen Me, has seen the Father ..."
"Before Abraham was, I am...." is a

koan. The Prologue of St. John's Gospel
is such a koan and above all: the very
figure of the Christ. However, manipulated
as an institutional stage prop, he remains
the Great Unknown: the riddle which the
West failed to solve, even failed to recognize
as its supreme koan.

The "wisdom of the East" with its
tempting exoticism is none other than the
universally human wisdom repressed in
the West, denatured by legalistic
Christianity, dogmatic Marxism, nihilistic
commercialism, and the myopia from
which they originate.

The detour via the East is not just a
fashion. It has become the shortest way home
for those many who, in their search for

Meaning, for values to live by, are dissatisfied
by and alienated from the religious programming of their upbringing. In the
Abrahamic traditions (Judaism, Christianity,
Islam) religious experience is by and large a
second-hand derivative from that of their
prophets and founders. Hinduism and
Buddhism allow a great diversity of experiencing, embrace a formidable variety of
spiritual pathways.

Both however culminate in that direct
Knowing, that transcendental insight, that
does not so much herald Salvation as that
it constitutes it.

When the primal religious questions,
these first signalings of the specifically
human impulse towards Reality/Truth
occur in the child: "Who am I?" "Who
are you?" "Why did my cat die?" "Where
is she now?" one might see this openness
to Reality/Truth as the birth of faith. I
would call this stage "Faith I."

At the end point of the inner human process, at the point of full "realization," one might speak of Faith III, a stage which may or may never be attained.

In the Interval between Faith I and III the impulse does not cease. In traditional societies it finds relief in the generally accepted symbol- and belief-systems of one's culture, of its exoteric religion. Faith expresses itself here in "beliefs" (Faith II). The believer finds confirmation and security in shared devotions, rituals, moral precepts. He gains a sense of belonging, finds support from the in-group and its collective group-ego.

This solidarity is in constant danger of the in-group ego's tendency to indulge in self-righteousness and megalomania. Especially in the Abrahamic religions it has, through the ages, caused endless persecutions, witchhunts, inquisitions, and massacres.

The inherited archetypal symbols, the great Myths which survive in even the most exoteric forms of religion, offer the believer the opportunity to break through the exoteric shell to its esoteric core, thus attaining Faith III in which Faith I and II are integrated.

"Believing" mutates into Knowing, all credulousness is overcome.

The Way to Faith III runs through all the great religious traditions. It may also be found to circumvent these.

The marginalization of the religious traditions in our time has turned the Interval between Faith I and Faith III into a desert in which the religious impulse finds itself tempted to follow the self-proclaimed dispensers of spiritual fast food, which only very temporarily still its hunger. This leads to a desperate *à la carte* spirituality, in which the confused victim becomes prone to chronic, promiscuous guru addiction, and if well-heeled to the jet pilgrimages of the New Age Deluxe industry.

Insofar as a symbol system encourages its devotees to see its symbols as fingers pointing at Reality/Truth, it is of inestimable worth. As such Buddhism not only allows but demands constant investigation of all its propositions and teachings. Where such a system demands being swallowed whole, moreover in linguistically obsolete formulations, it becomes totalitarian and bound to spawn intolerance, superstition, fanaticism and—as soon as coercion weakens—indifference, apostasy, cynicism.

Beware! To be irreverent to superstition arouses anger, to contradict it, fury.... Be ironical about it and make a deadly enemy....

It is wise to avoid militants of all plumage, to trust only the fanatically unfanatic.

From the viewpoint of *beliefs* all doubt is disastrous. From the viewpoint of *faith,* doubt is the indispensable stimulant.

To lose one's *beliefs* may not be a loss but a gain: an opportunity. "When the heart weeps for what it has lost, the spirit laughs for what it has gained," is an ancient Sufi saying.

To lose one's *faith,* however, is catastrophic; the loss of this vital human constituent means mutilation, dehumanization, cynicism, nihilism.

The contemporary crisis, not only of beliefs but of faith, gave birth to an era which, no longer merely post-Christian, threatens to become ever more post-Human.

What Saint Bonaventure called "the eye of flesh" and "the eye of reason" are both blind to the nature of Christ and Buddha. These seem only discernible to Bonaventure's "eye of contemplation" which, he says, is "onto liberation." Elsewhere known as "The Third Eye," "The Buddha Eye," it is no other than our physical eye, once it is awakened from looking-at to seeing.

It appears that only the Christ in humans is able to read and decode the Gospels, and that to the Ego—and particularly to the collective in-group ego—scripture is merely printed matter, all too often seditious printed matter, indispensable justification for hatred, intolerance, torture, pogrom, massacre.

The centuries are there to prove it.

Myths are stories or sequences of stories which express, in profoundly poetic form, inexpressible verities and Meanings, ungraspable to the intellect: If a myth which in the past conveyed such Meanings, no longer speaks to people, if the interaction between story and listener is broken, what was once a living myth becomes part of cultural history, becomes mythology.

To speak of the Christ Myth, the Marian Myth is no way derogatory, neither does it deny the historicity of Jesus of Nazareth or his mother.

Myth, symbol, nor work of art are in need of analysis, explanation, commentary. They have to be experienced, tasted. Johann Strauss did not write his waltzes for musicologists but for dancers, for lovers.

When myth is indoctrinated as if it were fact, when symbol is turned into concept by theological sophistry, religious experience is blocked instead of released, stimulated. What is being force fed is not living myth but mythology: the myth, no longer experienced, has been petrified into "belief."

Through the centuries the churches have preserved the Christ Myth, central to, and inextricably interwoven with, Western culture. This is their undeniable merit. They have, however, throughout history hidden behind it, not only co-habited with most anti-human structures, but covered them under religious foam while profiting from them. This is their eternal shame.

Buddhism, although relatively innocent of religious persecution and inquisition, cannot be acquitted from similar subservience to worldly power structures.

41

In order to clarify something, this personal reminiscence:

Raised in an agnostic family, I read one day, in later childhood, the Prologue to St. John's Gospel. "The Light that lighteneth every man come into the world" struck me with great force, echoed in me, somehow assured me as to my congenital human status, gave me a first glimpse into the riddle of human existence, into the inner human process....

Somehow in our Catholic town I must have heard the expression "Mystical Body of Christ," and read of The Fish being one of the oldest symbols of Christ. Letting these symbols play freely in my mind, I came to see the Mystical Body in the shape of a fish of cosmic proportions. Every scale on its immense body was a human face. This gigantic Cosmic Fish I saw as sailing through the interstellar spaces....

Much later, when the figures of Christ had become the paradigm of Fully Human, it was in Hwa Yen that I found the complementarity to my childhood vision of the Cosmic Fish: in the total interdependence, the mutual penetration, the self-identity of all beings.

Knowingly or unknowingly each one of us is at once, component and totality of the Cosmic Fish....

Originally the rite of baptism signified the radical turnabout of a person who renounced his old life to assume a new one. The rite did not transform him into a Christian, but into "a Christ" (*ein Christ*). In the Eucharist he partook of and in "the Christ's Body," the Specifically, Divinely, Human, confirming his belonging to the Cosmic Fish....

Mahayana points, as powerfully, at Rinzai's "True Man in this mass of red flesh." It does not seek to make one into a Buddhist, but into a Buddha: by liberating the Unborn, the Specifically Human, from ego's delusions.

Commitment to what the Cosmic
Fish embodied and Hwa Yen clarified, has
no essential connections with, nor implies
commitment to any authoritarian
Institution.

No one has ever isolated the Specifically
Human, the Unborn, in the laboratory,
but Rembrandt has painted it in all his
models, and supremely in the late self por-
traits; Bach has made it audible in
Magnificat, Passions, suites, fugues in a
hundred ways; a Yasujiro Ozu, a Bresson
have shown it cinematographically. That
which is deservedly called "great" in art, is
expression of It, evocation of It.

It is hard to understand how the
universal rite of the Eucharist, this affirma-
tion of the Truly Human, reciprocally and
with its Paradigm, could be so carefully
hemmed in by conditions enforced or set
by the Institution. However rationalized,
these conditions are almost certainly a

despotic perversion of the reality of the
Cosmic Fish, for It includes All....

Who lives and dies in Its Presence,
needs Buddha nor Jesus to save him. He
goes his way, he is his Way.

Essential Buddhism and essential
Christianity are both True-Man-isms:
transcendental, yet radically incarnational
humanisms.

Buddhology, Christology are then
either intrinsic anthropologies, or mere
theological constructs.

Jesus saves ... nobody until and
unless in some Emmaus or other he is
recognized as the risen Christ in the one
who accompanied us on the Way.

Pope John XXIII, it is generally
believed, died in 1963. By now, however, it
is clear that he did not. He is as alive as
ever....

In his last encyclical, "Pacem in Terris," he speaks of a "Law written on every human heart which his conscience enjoins him to obey...." "On the heart," said this pope, not merely on the paper of sacred books! He had seen that in the deepest hollow of the heart there is an immense force, a faith in life, in love, beyond all ideologies. He had seen the True Self, and this he lived.

He had learned, during his long service in Bulgaria, Turkey, Greece, France, between World Wars I and II, that the theological scientism of the left hemisphere (*theologia* *sinistra*...!) with its cerebral juggling of concepts, had contributed immensely to the massive alienation from the Church, and, beyond this, to the debility of the religious impulse, which eventually brought about its transfer to the idolatry of technology.

Dead concepts are not merely dead, they are deadly toxic.... John XXIII threw open the windows to get rid of the fumes.

He seemed confident that a freer association, in a contemporary mode, with the spiritual treasures and symbols of the Church would not endanger, but on the contrary stimulate authentic spirituality. This truly "religious orientation to existence" pervades all of his last encyclical, "Pacem in Terris"....

A pope who could quip: "How would I know? I am only the pope," who had overcome all the megalomania of ego, could not possibly take the group-ego of his senescent, all-male, all-knowing, sacrosanct apparatus all too seriously. In his spirit the Good News was not jammed by its collective ego's clamor. After centuries he once again showed the Other Face of the Church and of Christianity, that "Original Face" which church history has betrayed: the Specifically Human Face.

He saw clearly how the Institution had failed in its attempts to channel all of human life, to regulate the flow of all feeling, seeing, thinking and acting within compulsive dogmatic routines, how it had mistaken obsolete linguistic conventions for the essence of Tradition.

He understood that hierarchy is neither rejected nor mocked, provided it is clearly a hierarchy of values not merely proclaimed, but lived; and that authority is not denied insofar as it expresses Truth/Reality and hence manifests Wisdom and Compassion.

His own natural authority of the heart far exceeded the confines of his Church, and so he became a Pope for all Seasons, the prophet of human solidarity in our time.

"Pacem in Terris," as all that John XXIII said and did, carried the conviction that the religious attitude to all existence is indispensable to cope with the practical problems of hunger, armament trade, violence and war. Hence his openness to macro-ecumenism and a macro-ecological approach.

"Love thy neighbor ... " impossible a as command, is neither command nor impossible to the enlightened man. It is his inevitable mode of being. I see Angelo Roncalli as one who, having attained full awakening, refuses to enter Nirvana, but descends into the market place bestowing blessings, and guiding all beings to their Awakening.

I see him as a Christian Bodhisattva, or in Catholic terms: as the manifestation of the Holy Spirit in our century.

The windows are being forced shut now, but meanwhile there have been a Romero, a Helder Camara, a Mendez Arceo, a Huntshauser, a Tutu.... There are the living Basis Movements and numberless Latin American martyrs for a newly perceived humanness ... proving the aliveness of the Christ Myth, of the "Light the darkness cannot overcome," and of the Spirit that moved Angelo Roncalli.

Inter-religious dialogue is destined to remain fruitless unless based on intense and fearless intra-religious monologue, followed by a radically open witness to authentic religious experience.

Where, instead of the dialectic of concepts, a dialectic of experiencing and intuition is given its chance, inter-religious "dialogue" becomes that indispensable form of group therapy in which the pathological incriminations to which the inflated group-egos are subject, are quite naturally discounted and overcome.

What Matters

To the degree that the religious
traditions stand for Reality/Truth, they
are not in conflict with one another, nor
necessarily with scientific truth. They are,
however, in conflict in direct proportion to
the linguistic chauvinism, the cerebral
theological conceits, the pathological
narcissism of their group-egos.

On the exoteric level the traditions
are therefore irreconcilable. On the esoteric,
experiential level of the heart reigns and
eloquent, reverential silence.

All anxieties about the preservation
of "identity" betray the depth of delusion
of some group ego.

Contempt and animosity towards
"the others" is so ingrained, that we have
the greatest difficulty taking their spiritual
life seriously. Indoctrination is so persua-
sive that we can't help assuming that "they"
too are programmed, be it incorrectly.

As long as the non-Christian religions are considered as mere antipasto for the Last Supper, all macro-ecumenism is fraudulent.

When Hui Hai was asked: "Are Buddhism, Taoism and Confucianism three different religions or one and the same?" he answered:

"For men of the highest capacity they are one. For the mediocre they are three. For those below this level they are not only three, but irreconcilable.... Whether a man reaches liberation, however, depends on himself, not on differences in doctrine."

Buddhism, sometimes described as a merely philosophical and ethical system, has for millions through the centuries been the Way from primal ignorance to integration and enlightenment. Therefore, non-theistic as it is, it is surely a religion.

Far from being "pessimistic," Buddhism, especially Mahayana, is rooted in the absolute trust (faith!) that we humans embody the Specifically Human, the Buddha Nature, and moreover have the capacity to realize it in both the sense of being fully *aware of It,* but also in the sense of *actualizing It.* Far from being nihilistic, its pillars are the Great Compassion which is the Great Wisdom, the Great Wisdom which is the Great Compassion.

"It is the divine in man that justifies my belief in God," says Nicholas Berdyaev.

"Do you believe in God?"

"Which one, whose God?"

"Now, be serious please. Do you believe in God?"

"Seriously, I believe in nothing but That."

Proof of the existence of God....
Where Aquinas failed, Johann Sebastian
Bach succeeded without even trying....
Above the often tired, cloying, hateful texts
his music soars to Timeless Life.

About Eckhart's Godhead, about the
Void, Sunyata, I can speak without feeling
either fool or hypocrite. If I talk about a
personal God, I hear myself sound phony:
"God" is all too superannuated, too thoroughly polluted by too many scoundrels....
Still, when I speak *to* God—at times
one can't help oneself—He/She is
Absolutely Personal.

Western emphasis on Being, is balanced by Eastern stress on non-Being, the
Void. Both are complementary expressions
for what language lacks the tools to express:
opposing glimpses of Truth/Reality.
Awakening may be attained by either road
and, perhaps even more fully, by insight
into their absolute self-identity.

What in Buddhism is spoken of, in
the negative mode, as Sunyata, Absolute No-
Thingness, Emptiness, and articulated in
the positive mode as Suchness, Tathagata,
is the primal Mystery. Verbalized as *upaya*
(skillful stratagems), it is a stimulant to
contemplation.

The Transcendent is not "out there,"
not "up there," but on this side of the
Great Divide, Immanent in us at depths
unfathomably beyond the level of ego.

The Void, No-Thingness, Sunyata is not
an emptiness opposed to a fullness. It is that
Absolute Fullness that is the Ground of all
that is, its deepest Reality. "God is my
Ground, I am God's Ground," says Eckhart.

For the Christian, the Other Shore is
on the opposite bank of the Great Divide.
For the Buddhist the Other Shore is
Now/Here, the Transcendent is as immanent as the Immanent is transcendent.

The secular is sacred, for at each moment all Form is the manifestation of the Formless: Reality/Truth, its self-revelation. This self-revelation the Christ calls the "Father," with Whom he is one: "not-two."

It is not a matter of being "united" with God, but of being one with, unseparated from "I Am Who Am."

Where Eckhart speaks of Godhead, Nothing-ness, where Berdyaev says: "The Void from which I, but also God looms up ... out of the Divine Nothing the Creator was born," both are close to the Absolute NoThingness of essential Buddhism. This is an ideal example of inter-religious understanding on that profound level where it becomes possible, inevitable.

It is not the self-deprecating "I am nothing" that sets me free, but the insight that "NoThingness is Me": that I am a fleeting condensation of this NoThing, this really-Real that is unchanging in its pattern of uninterrupted change.

We have been immensely enriched, spiritually revitalized by the mystical traditions and insights of Asia, by the rehabilitation of what Leibniz, and after him Aldous Huxley, called "the perennial philosophy." What is heresy to the goose, may be spiritual rebirth to the gander.

There is no Christian, Buddhist, Hindu or Judaic truth. There is Truth/Reality and there is delusion.

It is not a matter of choosing between Christianity and Buddhism. They do not collide in me, they are complementary. This complementarity may be easier to understand to the upright Buddhist than to the more dogmatically programmed Christian believer.

Under the starry summer sky, hearing the song of the cicadas, musing on those I love, on this beloved earth, on living, on dying, I am a Buddhist. Going indoors, switching on the radio, glancing at the headlines, I hear His cry: "Why hast Thou forsaken Me?..."

To be committed to Truth/Reality does not carry any obligation to join any group, movement, church or party. Even less does it oblige me to any kind of religious, sectarian, ethnic, national, political self-labeling. It compels me to refrain from any such labeling and joining.

Convergences: "The Light that light-eneth every man," the "sleeping Christ within," Rinzai's "True Man," Bankei's "Unborn" may be seen as referring to that core of Supreme Sanity that is the very essence of our human reality. It is at any moment available at the price of abandoning ego delusions, by radical de-conditioning....

If the purpose of psychotherapy is the attainment of Sanity, it should aim at this radical de-conditioning. It would however require this Sanity first of all on the part of the self-appointed "therapist," with or without Ph.D.

What the Prologue of St. John's Gospel once awakened, what was later con-firmed in its own way by Eckhart, Hui Neng, Ramana Maharshi, Rinzai, the Heart Sutra, the Kegon Sutra, Thomas' Gospel—and at least as clearly—by all truly great art, is this Supreme Sanity, the Specifically Human genetically encoded in us.

Dogmas, rituals and formulas may then be considered as road signs, as fingers pointing to, as upaya towards, this Supreme Sanity.

Zen, it is said, is that which outside of all scriptures points directly at the True Self, the Specifically Human. It can only be transmitted from heart to heart.

"Zen" then, may be that which in the religious traditions is the truly, essentially "religious" ingredient that is trans-religious and trans-cultural.

The Zen experience is the im-mediate existential contact with the really-Real, with the innermost workings of life, with existence-as-such. It is the recovery of our ever-obscured Supreme Sanity.

What Christ and Buddha toiled to transmit from heart to heart, makes it unlikely that either was under the illusion of starting a mass movement.

"Cleave the wood and thou shalt find
Me....

"Lift the stone and I am there ..." says
Jesus in the Gospel according to Thomas.

Dogen (13th c.) answers:

"All beings *are* the Buddha Nature.

"Buddha Nature is impermanence."
It is as if both together could say in unison
what the Christ in the Gospel according to
Thomas answered to the question:

"Where did you come from?"

"From the Light where the Light
originated through Itself."

The Buddha says: "I am the Eye of
the World."

The Christ says: "I am the Light of
the World." Where they say I, it is the I of
all the Masters: the totally alive "not-I,"
the "not-Me" of Bankei's Unborn, of
St. John's Light.

"The Buddha is the Essence of your
being, outside of it, there is no Buddha."

—Hui Neng

Reading of spiritual texts, of scriptures, does not "reveal" so much as "remind" me of what the Unborn knew from the beginningless past. Once it becomes merely habitual, addictive, it may cause reverential blindness, does not remind me any more, but blocks fresh perception.

The epithet "syncretism" must not be used judgmentally, unless reserved for indiscriminate and philistine scrambling of incongruent religious concepts and rituals. No tradition is simon-pure. Christianity appropriated and integrated Greek, Roman and countless other elements.

"Heresy," once exceptional and punishable is, since the convergences, counterparts and isomorphisms in the religious traditions have grown so obvious, no longer heresy but an experiential way to find the spiritual home suited to one's temperament. Concepts that clash in the brain, may become living insights that fuse in the heart.

The all too real heresy of our time is that alienation from the profundity of human life, of which the advance guard is that Scientism/Technology which, ignoring Reality/Truth, takes all that defies objectification as objectifiable and even quantifiable. Oddly, its rear guard is that fundamentalism which recycles scriptural clichés as the solution to all existential problems, that objectifies the Ultimately Unobjectifiable into a sacrosanct Thing.

Science/Technology's "practical" viewpoint justifies the manipulation of all that is, without even suspecting its Value. Immensely active, inventive, energetic, ruthless, it acts as if the earth and its inhabitants stood waiting to be man-handled: "Those thousand-year-old oaks? A cinch for the chainsaw.... That fertile valley over there? Flood it, build a dam, order the turbines...!"

The opposite of faith as an openness to Reality/Truth is neither unbelief, skepticism nor doubt. It is the un-faith, the anti-faith that characterizes the syndrome of Nihilism.

Modern Nihilism is that highly struc-tured anti-faith, which like a submarine earthquake has undermined all religious and spiritual values as well as all the classical humanistic ones: veracity, fair play, con-stancy, tolerance, compassion, generosity, not to mention honor and nobility. It destroys the roots, it poisons the wells, it subverts the ground on which human life, culture, community are possible.

Nihilism ignores all criteria of what it means to be human, pre-human, sub-human, anti-human. In its massive rejection of the human dimension, it has, as successor to the Post-Christian era, ushered in the Post-human era.

The idols of this all pervading anti-faith are "logic": nationalism, racism, pan-economic obsession with greed, a technology running amuck. Not the slightest heresy is tolerated. Behind the Curtain heretics were interned in asylums. In the "Free World," they are, provisionally, not burned but fired.

Triumphant in the West, Nihilism is colonizing, that is Westernizing, the Third World, uprooting autochtonic traditions and cultures, destroying the ties of peoples to their earth, their traditional and agricultural and economic systems. It reduces entire populations to the condition of a permanent sub-proletariat, enslaved to multinational power structures.

Nihilism is at the opposite pole of "Reverence for Life." It has reverence for nothing except for its own anti-values of power, public relations, lies, short-term profit.

Nihilistic rhetoric and rationalization, however, is replete with the choicest altruistic, patriotic, moralistic terminology. The symbol "God" is abused with such fervor and frequency that it has lost all credibility.

In our nihilistic chaos every national, every ideological collectivity has dishonored itself utterly. Gulag, gas chamber, torture cellar, apartheid, induced famine, nuclear holocaust, have routinely been justified with an ad hoc gnosis of ideological twaddle and demonic hypocrisy.

Modern Nihilism hides behind innumerable masks: political, economic, artistic, psychological, religious. The task of the unmasking of Nihilism demands absolute priority if we are to survive. This requires enormous inter-disciplinary skills and is therefore a collective task.

All consistent egocentricity is insane.
Nihilism is the collective and endemic
form of this insanity.

Whosoever, by ineffable grace, or
sheer good luck, has survived this century
of insanity, of Hitler, Stalin, Idi Amin,
Papa Doc, Pinochet, of Auschwitz and
Hiroshima, of Bhopals and Love Canals,
yet still underestimates the contagious
virus of Nihilism as Absolute Evil, hardly
merits his survival.

Lord Acton stands corrected:
"Absolute Avidya + Absolute Power =
Absolute Evil."

The difference between "democratic"
and "totalitarian" Nihilism is the difference
in semantics, in ritual, in rhetoric and in
categories of victims.

A much abridged symptomatology of modern Nihilism would include: disregard and detachment of all values except the immediate satisfaction of narcissistic, individual and herd impulses ... atrophy of all notions of relatedness and responsibility to other humans, to animals, plants, the earth ... degeneracy of the sense of beauty, truth, goodness, humanness, hence total mistrust of disinterested service ... degradation of all fellow beings to the status of Things ... progressive debility of all the higher functions by unrelenting and total bedevilment by electronic noise and imagery, media trivia, spectator sports, laugh shows, quizzes, commercials, propaganda for whiskeys, presidents, celebrities, gadgets, space trips.... Unavoidable consequences: alienation from self and environment—consumer addiction—identity crisis—existential vacuum—depression—mass psychosis—violence—sexual depravity—drug and alcohol addiction—teenage and all other categories of suicide, including our own's collective incubation.

Where the Dow replaces the Tao, all of Life becomes desecrated.

It is naive to blame technology-as-such for our, and the Earth's misfortune. Modern technology is unthinkable without its empowerment by the mega-financial/pan-economic/military complex. Technology thrives on this, and in symbiosis with it created that *Twin Fetish* which deserves the title of the *Satanic Tremendum.*

One could imagine a technology empowered by Wisdom/Compassion with as immense a constructive potential as that of the Twin Fetish is all-destructive.

It would be a technology in symbiosis with the earth and its inhabitants instead of being antagonistic to it, hence suicidal.

Where there is a Tremendum, there must be a *Fascinosum*.... The massive conditioning apparatus by which the Twin Fetish wields its power: the media, with their obscene advertising, television which makes the world as flat as its screen and indulges in the pseudo-festive jollification and continuous celebration of the shenanigans of the Twin Fetish, plays the part of the *Fascinosum:*

Will Bomb, poisoning of the biosphere, or the collective de-sensitization by televised toxic waste products spell the demise of the Human?

Lest this should be dismissed as leftist anti-capitalism: there is an enormous difference between what used to be called capitalism and the unrestrained power of faceless mammoth corporations, which flout all ethical considerations, dominate governments, despoil the earth, feed children carcinogens, release chemical and radio-active poison without flinching: Satanic Tremendum.

Before World War II Americans had full trust in the ethical standards of their great corporations. Today only few are unaware of the Twin Fetish's contempt for and faceless disregard of all decency, of corporate criminality as an ever present fact of life. Beginning awakening?

Peace, that passionate universal longing, is neither a matter of international politics, nor a miracle to be hoped for by the propitiation and mollification of the Twin Fetish.

It is a matter of worldwide awakening to the galloping malignancy of the *Satanic Tremendum,* of a new intensified awareness of what is Human and what is less than that.

Millions of people are tortured, killed, deported, kidnapped, starved. Numberless children are dying today, and we prattle of peace....

"Peace is not an absence of war."
Spinoza said it, but it is mindlessly quoted
out of context, for he added, "it is a virtue,
a state of mind, a disposition for
benevolence, confidence, justice."

"It is each person's responsibility to
free himself from the errors of his time."
                                    —Marguerite Yourcenar

"What is your name?" Enem asked
Ejaku.
"My name is Enem!" Ejaku replied
"Now, wait a moment! Enem that's
me! I am Enem!"
"OK," said Ejaku, "in that case I'm
Ejaku!"
And both roared with laughter.
                                    —a Zen Koan

There is no I, no other....

Miraculously, in the face of the uninterrupted programming which violates the
inner life, the "inner principle of the unity

73

"*On a trip on the Ogowe River in 1915 it came to me that reverence for life is the only basis on which a viable ethic can be built....*"

—ALBERT SCHWEITZER

of all knowledge and all the activities of our social and spiritual being" (Tagore), is being retrieved. Ever more articulate counter currents of awareness and atonement give hope: the spirit may yet take wing where the poison has reached its saturation point. A "New Order" does indeed manifest itself in many ways, be it in still embryonic form.

It would be unrealistic to expect, or even to hope, these counter currents to grow sufficiently and in time to prevent the disappearing forever of all human life, with hydrogen bang or pollution whimper; without leaving a trace of the Human experiment in all its horror but also of its grandeur: of Christ and Buddha, of Chuang Tzu and Lao Tze, of all the artists, the celebrants of the Human, of the Earth, of sheer Being, the buildings of Parthenon, Angkor Wat, Chartres; of Mozart, Rilke, Leonardo, Rodin, of Angelo Roncalli, Albert Schweitzer....

Is perhaps a technological/economic/
medical catastrophe or plague, needed—
one of providentially still barely manageable
proportions—to act as a catalyst for that
worldwide awakening, that metanoia in
which the Will to Power mutates into that
Will to Meaning which will not only
justify human survival, but grant it its
last chance?

*This little compendium was written
as a self-confrontation, to be shared with a
few of my natural friends.... One of these
read it and challenged me to compress, in a
page or two, "That Which Matters" in its
most naked essence. It was the risk I took! At
even greater risk I shall insert this provisional
diagnosis of our reality situation. It claims no
originality whatsoever, as, obviously, I am
influenced by years of free association with
Western and Oriental insights:*

What in negative, minor key is spoken of as Emptiness, the Void Sunyata, as
"Oriental Nothingness" (Hisamatsu) or
"Absolute Nothingness" (Nishitani), and
in the major key, the positive mode, as
Suchness, as Buddha Nature, is beyond
the limits of what language has the tools to
 express. It is a way of saying: "Be silent for
this is the Primal Mystery!"

This Primal Mystery can be glimpsed,
but only by pure experiencing, as That
from Which all that is, is perceived to
loom up, and into Which, at the end of its
existence—time—to flow back.

What one is likely to lose sight of is
that during this existence-time, I—as all
things and beings—am never anything but
a temporary "condensation" of this Absolute
Nothingness, this Primal Mystery. Yet, it is
during this brief span of existence in time,
that I must live the timeless—that is: "eter-
nity." Mere condensation that I am, I am
no phantom, I am real, and have the

capacity to watch the entire, eternal Cosmic
drama of the Formless condensing itself
into Form, yet remaining Itself.

As I watch this drama, played in my
own flesh and in the world around me, the
true relationship of "I, Thou and It,"
reveals itself as being embedded, contained
in the Primal Mystery.

The micro-moment of awareness
that my eye truly meets your eye, that the
"condensation" of Nothingness which I
call *"Me"* embraces that condensation I
call *"You,"* is the moment of Truth, of the
Fullness of Life, beyond love, beyond
friendship.

In the timeless micro-moment
(Chinese *nen,* Sanskrit *ksana*) of Truth, in
this absolute Now, past and future are
cancelled: it is the epiphany of the Real, in
which I see: I am neither I nor other.

"In Him we live and have our being" is an understatement. In the Clear Light of this epiphany: issued from, suffused by, Absolute Nothingness, I remain forever unseparated from It in my being/ non-being.

"God's Ground is my Ground" says Eckhart and indeed: God and I are one another's exuviae.... Another understatement is that self-noughting: "I am just a nothing." On the contrary: "Nothingness is me!"

The timeless moment of seeing the Real is the moment of the Christ's Resurrection, of Communion with the Cosmic Christ. It is the birth moment of the Specifically Human: seeing the Buddha Nature being born out of the "womb of Buddhahood," the Tathatagharba.

The flash of experiencing this epiphany,
may utter itself in a birthcry that is at once
roar of raucous laughter and moan of deepest
pain, bitterest of tears. For in this flash all
the insanity of our world, the cruel farce of
"History" appears as being as wildly comical
as the appalling suffering which its folly,
greed and anger inflict on all that lives on
earth, is beyond all sadness.

This century of immense know-how and
total ignorance of know-why, its unbroken
succession of virtuosi of mass murder, of that
Satanic Tremendum *that radically denies*
the mutual interdependence of all that lives
on the planet, has denied millions of starved,
murdered, humans their chance of attaining
the endpoint of their human pilgrimage, has
desecrated all the biosphere.

Such total triumph of Avidya *over*
Wisdom/Compassion such sin against the Holy
Spirit, may well signal—beyond the final
failure of the cosmic Experiment Man—the
impending extinction of Homosaurus Sapiens.

Could it be that the swift alternation, each day, of overwhelming beauty and tenderness with unspeakable cruelty, stupidity, horror and evil is the only spiritual discipline we need—provided all the senses are kept open, no moodlifters taken—to awaken to the great Guru, the Master within?

Yes!

... Life is what it is about:
I want no truck with death.
If we were not so singleminded
about keeping our lives moving,
and for once could do nothing,
perhaps a huge silence
might interrupt this sadness
of never understanding ourselves
and of threatening ourselves with death.
Perhaps the earth can teach us
as when everything seems dead
and later proves to be alive....

       —Pablo Neruda

If I have no more than a day to live,
let it be a hundred years long, then let me
die as a Human Being....

MAY ALL BEINGS BE FULFILLED

Last Judgment

Looking back as far as I can, seeing myself
as a newborn baby, I was still pre-human, a
hominid, an anthropoid, but with the
built-in potentiality—or rather the assign-
ment, the task—to become fully Human.

The degree to which I have grown
Human—in the full sense of the word—
defines whether my task has been fulfilled.
If not, I have lived in vain.

About the Author

Frederick Franck served as a doctor on Albert Schweitzer's staff in Africa. He is the author of the bestseller *My Days with Albert Schweitzer,* the classic *The Zen of Seeing,* and *Zen Seeing, Zen Drawing.* The only official artist for Vatican II, his drawings and paintings are in the collections of a score of museums including MOMA and the Whitney, and his sculptures are installed in religious and secular institutions around the world. He lives in Warwick, New York, where he has converted an eighteenth-century mill ruin into a transreligious sanctuary called Pacem in Terris.

Also by Frederick Franck

Days with Albert Schweitzer
African Sketchbook
My Eye Is in Love
Outsider in the Vatican
I Love Life
Exploding Church
Simenon's Paris
The Zen of Seeing
Fingers Pointing toward the Sacred
The Book of Angelus Silesius
Everyone: The Timeless Myth of Everyman Reborn
Zen and Zen Classics: Selections from R. H. Blyth
The Awakened Eye
Art as a Way
The Buddha Eye
The Supreme Koan
The Tao of the Cross
Life Drawing Life
To Be Human against All Odds
Zen Seeing, Zen Drawing
Watching the Vatican
What Does It Mean to Be Human?
Pacem in Terris, A Love Story
Moments of Seeing
Seeing Venice—An Eye in Love
A Passion for Seeing
A Zen Book of Hours

About SKYLIGHT PATHS Publishing

SkyLight Paths Publishing is creating a place where people of different spiritual traditions come together for challenge and inspiration, a place where we can help each other understand the mystery that lies at the heart of our existence.

Through spirituality, our religious beliefs are increasingly becoming a part of our lives—rather than *apart* from our lives. While many of us may be more interested than ever in spiritual growth, we may be less firmly planted in traditional religion. Yet, we to want to deepen our relationship to the sacred, to learn from our own as well as from other faith traditions, and to practice in new ways.

SkyLight Paths sees both believers and seekers as a community that increasingly transcends traditional boundaries of religion and denomination—people wanting to learn from each other, *walking together, finding the way.*

We at SkyLight Paths take great care to produce beautiful books that present meaningful spiritual content in a form that reflects the art of making high quality books. Therefore, we want to acknowledge those who contributed to the production of this book.

PRODUCTION
Sara Dismukes & Tim Holtz

EDITORIAL
Amanda Dupuis, Maura D. Shaw
& Emily Wichland

JACKET DESIGN
Sara Dismukes

TEXT DESIGN
Tim Holtz

PRINTING & BINDING
Friesens Corporation, Manitoba, Canada

Other Interesting Books—Spirituality

Lighting the Lamp of Wisdom
A Week Inside an Ashram
by *John Ittner*; foreword by *Dr. David Frawley*

This insider's guide to Hindu spiritual life takes you into a typical week of retreat inside an ashram to demystify the ashram experience and show you what to expect from your own visit. Includes a discussion of worship services, meditation and yoga classes, chanting and music, work practice, and more.

6 x 9, 192 pp, b/w photographs, Quality PB, ISBN 1-893361-52-7 **$15.95**;
HC, ISBN 1-893361-37-3 **$24.95**

Waking Up
A Week Inside a Zen Monastery
by *Jack Maguire*; foreword by *John Daido Loori, Roshi*

An essential guide to what it's like to spend a week inside a Zen Buddhist monastery.

6 x 9, 224 pp, b/w photographs, Quality PB, ISBN 1-893361-55-1 **$16.95**;
HC, ISBN 1-893361-13-6 **$21.95**

Making a Heart for God
A Week Inside a Catholic Monastery
by *Dianne Aprile*; foreword by *Brother Patrick Hart*, OCSO

This essential guide to experiencing life in a Catholic monastery takes you to the Abbey of Gethsemani—the Trappist monastery in Kentucky that was home to author Thomas Merton—to explore the details. "More balanced and informative than the popular *The Cloister Walk* by Kathleen Norris." —*Choice: Current Reviews for Academic Libraries*

6 x 9, 224 pp, b/w photographs, Quality PB, ISBN 1-893361-49-7 **$16.95**;
HC, ISBN 1-893361-14-4 **$21.95**

Come and Sit
A Week Inside Meditation Centers
by *Marcia Z. Nelson*; foreword by *Wayne Teasdale*

The insider's guide to meditation in a variety of different spiritual traditions. Traveling through Buddhist, Hindu, Christian, Jewish, and Sufi traditions, this essential guide takes you to different meditation centers to meet the teachers and students and learn about the practices, demystifying the meditation experience.

6 x 9, 224 pp, b/w photographs, Quality PB, ISBN 1-893361-35-7 **$16.95**

Spiritual Practice

Finding Grace at the Center
The Beginning of Centering Prayer, 25th Anniversary Edition
by *M. Basil Pennington,* OCSO, *Thomas Keating,* OCSO, and *Thomas E. Clarke,* SJ
The book that helped launch the Centering Prayer "movement." Explains the prayer of *The Cloud of Unknowing,* posture and relaxation, the three simple rules of centering prayer, and how to cultivate centering prayer throughout all aspects of your life.
5 x 7¼, 112 pp, HC, ISBN 1-893361-69-1 **$14.95**

Three Gates to Meditation Practice
A Personal Journey into Sufism, Buddhism, and Judaism
by *David A. Cooper*

> Shows us how practicing within more than one spiritual tradition can lead us to our true home.

Here are over fifteen years from the journey of "post-denominational rabbi" David A. Cooper, author of *God Is a Verb,* and his wife, Shoshana—years in which the Coopers explored a rich variety of practices, from chanting Sufi *dhikr* to Buddhist Vipassanā meditation, to the study of kabbalah and esoteric Judaism. Their experience demonstrates that the spiritual path is really completely within our reach, whoever we are, whatever we do—as long as we are willing to practice it.
5½ x 8½, 240 pp, Quality PB, ISBN 1-893361-22-5 **$16.95**

Praying with Our Hands: *Twenty-One Practices of Embodied Prayer from the World's Spiritual Traditions*
by *Jon M. Sweeney;* photographs by *Jennifer J. Wilson;*
foreword by *Mother Tessa Bielecki;* afterword by *Taitetsu Unno, Ph.D.*

> A spiritual guidebook for bringing prayer into our bodies.

This inspiring book of reflections and accompanying photographs shows us twenty-one simple ways of using our hands to speak to God, to enrich our devotion and ritual. All express the various approaches of the world's religious traditions to bringing the body into worship. Spiritual traditions represented include Anglican, Sufi, Zen, Roman Catholic, Yoga, Shaker, Hindu, Jewish, Pentecostal, Eastern Orthodox, and many others.
8 x 8, 96 pp, 22 duotone photographs, Quality PB, ISBN 1-893361-16-0 **$16.95**

Labyrinths from the Outside In
Walking to Spiritual Insight—a Beginner's Guide
by *Donna Schaper* and *Carole Ann Camp*

> The user-friendly, interfaith guide to making and using labyrinths—for meditation, prayer, and celebration.

Labyrinth walking is a spiritual exercise *anyone* can do. This accessible guide unlocks the mysteries of the labyrinth for all of us, providing ideas for using the labyrinth walk for prayer, meditation, and celebrations to mark the most important moments in life. Includes instructions for making a labyrinth of your own and finding one in your area.
6 x 9, 208 pp, b/w illus. and photographs, Quality PB, ISBN 1-893361-18-7 **$16.95**

Spiritual Biography

The Life of Evelyn Underhill
An Intimate Portrait of the Groundbreaking Author of Mysticism
by *Margaret Cropper;* foreword by *Dana Greene*

Evelyn Underhill was a passionate writer and teacher who wrote elegantly on mysticism, worship, and devotional life. This is the story of how she made her way toward spiritual maturity, from her early days of agnosticism to the years when her influence was felt throughout the world.

6 x 9, 288 pp, 5 b/w photos, Quality PB, ISBN 1-893361-70-5 **$18.95**

Zen Effects: *The Life of Alan Watts*
by *Monica Furlong*

The first and only full-length biography of one of the most charismatic spiritual leaders of the twentieth century—now back in print!

Through his widely popular books and lectures, Alan Watts (1915–1973) did more to introduce Eastern philosophy and religion to Western minds than any figure before or since. Here is the only biography of this charismatic figure, who served as Zen teacher, Anglican priest, lecturer, academic, entertainer, a leader of the San Francisco renaissance, and author of more than thirty books, including *The Way of Zen, Psychotherapy East and West* and *The Spirit of Zen.*

6 x 9, 264 pp, Quality PB, ISBN 1-893361-32-2 **$16.95**

Simone Weil: *A Modern Pilgrimage*
by *Robert Coles*

The extraordinary life of the spiritual philosopher who's been called both saint and madwoman.

The French writer and philosopher Simone Weil (1906–1943) devoted her life to a search for God—while avoiding membership in organized religion. Robert Coles' intriguing study of Weil details her short, eventful life, and is an insightful portrait of the beloved and controversial thinker whose life and writings influenced many (from T. S. Eliot to Adrienne Rich to Albert Camus), and continue to inspire seekers everywhere.

6 x 9, 208 pp, Quality PB, ISBN 1-893361-34-9 **$16.95**

Mahatma Gandhi: *His Life and Ideas*
by *Charles F. Andrews;* foreword by *Dr. Arun Gandhi*

An intimate biography of one of the greatest social and religious reformers of the modern world.

Examines from a contemporary Christian activist's point of view the religious ideas and political dynamics that influenced the birth of the peaceful resistance movement, the primary tool that Gandhi and the people of his homeland would use to gain India its freedom from British rule. An ideal introduction to the life and life's work of this great spiritual leader.

6 x 9, 336 pp, 5 b/w photos, Quality PB, ISBN 1-893361-89-6 **$18.95**

SkyLight Illuminations
Andrew Harvey, series editor

Offers today's spiritual seeker an enjoyable entry into the classic texts of the world's spiritual traditions. Each is presented in an accessible translation, with facing pages of guided commentary from experts, giving you the keys you need to understand the history, context, and meaning of the text. This series enables readers of all backgrounds to experience and understand classic spiritual texts directly, and to make them a part of their lives.

Rumi and Islam—Selections from his Stories, Poems, and Discourses: *Annotated & Explained*
Translation and annotation by *Dr. Ibrahim Gamard*

Sheds new light on the religion of Rumi through a satisfying taste of Islamic Sufi mysticism.

Offers a new way of thinking about Rumi's poetry. Ibrahim Gamard focuses on Rumi's place within the Sufi tradition of Islam, providing readers with an image of the mystical side of the religion—one that has love of God at its core and sublime wisdom teachings as its pathways.
5½ x 8½, 240 pp, Quality PB, ISBN 1-59473-002-4 **$15.99**

Dhammapada: *Annotated & Explained*
Translation by *Max Müller;* annotation by *Jack Maguire*

The most beloved of all the Buddhist scriptures.

The Dhammapada—words spoken by the Buddha himself over 2,500 years ago—is notoriously difficult to understand for the first-time reader. Now you can experience the Dhammapada with understanding even if you have no previous knowledge of Buddhism. Enlightening facing-page commentary explains all the names, terms and references, giving you deeper insight into the text. An excellent introduction to Buddhist life and practice.
5½ x 8½, 160 pp, Quality PB, ISBN 1-893361-42-X **$14.95**

Zohar: *Annotated & Explained*
Translation and annotation by *Daniel C. Matt*

The cornerstone text of Kabbalah, now with facing-page commentary that illuminates and explains the text for you.

The best-selling author of *The Essential Kabbalah* brings together in one place the most important teachings of the *Zohar*, the canonical text of Jewish mystical tradition. Guides readers step by step through the midrash, mystical fantasy and Hebrew scripture that make up the *Zohar*, explaining the inner meanings in facing-page commentary. Ideal for readers without any prior knowledge of Jewish mysticism.
5½ x 8½, 176 pp, Quality PB, ISBN 1-893361-51-9 **$15.95**

SkyLight Illuminations

Andrew Harvey, series editor

Selections from the Gospel of Sri Ramakrishna
Annotated & Explained

Translation by *Swami Nikhilananda;* annotation by *Kendra Crossen Burroughs*

The words of India's greatest example of God-consciousness and mystical ecstasy in recent history.

Introduces the fascinating world of the Indian mystic and the universal appeal of his message that has inspired millions of devotees for more than a century. Selections from the original text and insightful yet unobtrusive commentary highlight the most important and inspirational teachings. Ideal for readers without any prior knowledge of Hinduism.

5½ x 8½, 240 pp, b/w photographs, Quality PB, ISBN 1-893361-46-2 **$16.95**

Hasidic Tales: *Annotated & Explained*

Translation and annotation by *Rabbi Rami Shapiro*

The legendary tales of the impassioned Hasidic rabbis.

The allegorical quality of Hasidic tales can be perplexing. Here, they are presented as stories rather than parables, making them accessible and meaningful. Each demonstrates the spiritual power of unabashed joy, offers lessons for leading a holy life, and reminds us that the Divine can be found in the everyday. Annotations explain theological concepts, introduce major characters, and clarify references unfamiliar to most readers.

5½ x 8½, 240 pp, Quality PB, ISBN 1-893361-86-1 **$16.95**

The Way of a Pilgrim: *Annotated & Explained*

Translation and annotation by *Gleb Pokrovsky*

This delightful account is the story of one man who sets out to learn the prayer of the heart—also known as the "Jesus prayer"—and how the practice transforms his existence. This edition guides you through the text with facing-page annotations explaining names, terms, and references.

5½ x 8½, 160 pp, b/w illustrations, Quality PB, ISBN 1-893361-31-4 **$14.95**

Bhagavad Gita: *Annotated & Explained*

Translation by *Shri Purohit Swami;* annotation by *Kendra Crossen Burroughs*

"The very best Gita for first-time readers." —Ken Wilber

Millions of people turn daily to India's most beloved holy book, whose universal appeal has made it popular with non-Hindus and Hindus alike. This edition introduces readers to the characters; explains references and philosophical terms; shares the interpretations of famous spiritual leaders and scholars; and more.

5½ x 8½, 192 pp, Quality PB, ISBN 1-893361-28-4 **$16.95**

Spirituality

Releasing the Creative Spirit: *Unleash the Creativity in Your Life*
by *Dan Wakefield*

From the author of *How Do We Know When It's God?*— a practical guide to accessing creative power in every area of your life.

Explodes the myths associated with the creative process and shows how everyone can uncover and develop their natural ability to create. Drawing on religion, psychology, and the arts, Dan Wakefield teaches us that the key to creation of any kind is clarity—of body, mind, and spirit—and he provides practical exercises that each of us can do to access that centered quality that allows creativity to shine. "Will help you find the source of your own spiritual and creative powers." —*Yoga Journal*
7 x 10, 256 pp, Quality PB, ISBN 1-893361-36-5 **$16.95**

The Alphabet of Paradise: *An A–Z of Spirituality for Everyday Life*
by *Howard Cooper*

One of the most eloquent new voices in spirituality, Howard Cooper takes us on a journey of discovery—into ourselves and into the past—to find the signposts that can help us live more meaningful lives. In twenty-six engaging chapters—from A to Z—Cooper spiritually illuminates the subjects of daily life, using an ancient Jewish mystical method of interpretation that reveals both the literal and more allusive meanings of each. Topics include: Awe, Bodies, Creativity, Dreams, Emotions, Sports, and more.
5 x 7¾, 224 pp, Quality PB, ISBN 1-893361-80-2 **$16.95**

Winter: *A Spiritual Biography of the Season*
Edited by *Gary Schmidt* and *Susan M. Felch*; illustrations by *Barry Moser*

Explore how the dormancy of winter can be a time of spiritual preparation and transformation.

In thirty stirring pieces, *Winter* delves into the varied feelings that winter conjures in us, calling up both the barrenness and the beauty of the natural world in wintertime. Includes selections by Will Campbell, Rachel Carson, Annie Dillard, Donald Hall, Ron Hansen, Jane Kenyon, Jamaica Kincaid, Barry Lopez, Kathleen Norris, John Updike, E. B. White, and many others. "This outstanding anthology features top-flight nature and spirituality writers on the fierce, inexorable season of winter.... Remarkably lively and warm, despite the icy subject." —★*Publishers Weekly* Starred Review
6 x 9, 288 pp, 6 b/w illus., Quality PB, ISBN 1-893361-92-6 **$18.95**;
HC, ISBN 1-893361-53-5 **$21.95**

Religious Etiquette/Reference

How to Be a Perfect Stranger, 3rd Edition
The Essential Religious Etiquette Handbook
Edited by *Stuart M. Matlins* and *Arthur J. Magida*

The indispensable guidebook to help the well-meaning guest when visiting other people's religious ceremonies.

A straightforward guide to the rituals and celebrations of the major religions and denominations in the United States and Canada from the perspective of an interested guest of any other faith, based on information obtained from authorities of each religion. Belongs in every living room, library, and office.

COVERS:

African American Methodist Churches • Assemblies of God • Baha'i • Baptist • Buddhist • Christian Church (Disciples of Christ) • Christian Science (Church of Christ, Scientist) • Churches of Christ • Episcopalian and Anglican • Hindu • Islam • Jehovah's Witnesses • Jewish • Lutheran • Mennonite/Amish • Methodist • Mormon (Church of Jesus Christ of Latter-day Saints) • Native American/First Nations • Orthodox Churches • Pentecostal Church of God • Presbyterian • Quaker (Religious Society of Friends) • Reformed Church in America/Canada • Roman Catholic • Seventh-day Adventist • Sikh • Unitarian Universalist • United Church of Canada • United Church of Christ

6 x 9, 432 pp, Quality PB, ISBN 1-893361-67-5 **$19.95**

Also available:

The Perfect Stranger's Guide to Funerals and Grieving Practices
A Guide to Etiquette in Other People's Religious Ceremonies
Edited by *Stuart M. Matlins*
6 x 9, 240 pp, Quality PB, ISBN 1-893361-20-9 **$16.95**

The Perfect Stranger's Guide to Wedding Ceremonies
A Guide to Etiquette in Other People's Religious Ceremonies
Edited by *Stuart M. Matlins*
6 x 9, 208 pp, Quality PB, ISBN 1-893361-19-5 **$16.95**

Other Interesting Books—Spirituality

Journeys of Simplicity: Traveling Light with Thomas Merton, Bashō, Edward Abbey, Annie Dillard & Others
by *Philip Harnden*

Offers vignettes of forty "travelers" and the few ordinary things they carried with them—from place to place, from day to day, from birth to death. What Thoreau took to Walden Pond. What Thomas Merton packed for his final trip to Asia. What Annie Dillard keeps in her writing tent. What an impoverished cook served M. F. K. Fisher for dinner. Much more. "'Herein you'll find sage, sly, wonderfully subversive advice." —Bill McKibben, author of *The End of Nature* and *Enough*
5 x 7¼, 128 pp, HC, ISBN 1-893361-76-4 **$16.95**

The Sacred Art of Listening
Forty Reflections for Cultivating a Spiritual Practice
by *Kay Lindahl*; illustrations by *Amy Schnapper*

More than ever before, we need to embrace the skills and practice of listening. You will learn to: Speak clearly from your heart • Communicate with courage and compassion • Heighten your awareness for deep listening • Enhance your ability to listen to people with different belief systems.
8 x 8, 160 pp, Illus., Quality PB, ISBN 1-893361-44-6 **$16.95**

Spiritual Innovators: Seventy-Five Extraordinary People Who Changed the World in the Past Century
Edited by *Ira Rifkin* and *the Editors at SkyLight Paths*;
foreword by *Dr. Robert Coles*

Dorothy Day, Black Elk, H. H. the Dalai Lama, Abraham Joshua Heschel, Krishnamurti, C. S. Lewis, Thomas Merton, Aimee Semple McPherson, Martin Luther King, Jr., Rabindranath Tagore, Simone Weil, and many more.

Profiles of the most important spiritual leaders of the past one hundred years. An invaluable reference of twentieth-century religion and an inspiring resource for spiritual challenge today. Authoritative list of seventy-five includes mystics and martyrs, intellectuals and charismatics from the East and West. For each, includes a brief biography, inspiring quotes and resources for more in-depth study.
6 x 9, 304 pp, b/w photographs, Quality PB, ISBN 1-893361-50-0 **$16.95**;
HC, ISBN 1-893361-43-8 **$24.95**

Or phone, fax, mail, or e-mail to: SKYLIGHT PATHS Publishing
Sunset Farm Offices, Route 4 • P.O. Box 237 • Woodstock, Vermont 05091
Tel: (802) 457-4000   Fax: (802) 457-4004   www.skylightpaths.com
Credit card orders: (800) 962-4544 (8:30AM–5:30PM ET Monday–Friday)
Generous discounts on quantity orders. Satisfaction guaranteed. Prices subject to change.